t

Internet

Linda Ingham

WILLOW
ISLAND
EDITIONS

Dedication
To Mother,
who bravely went online at the age of 82

Microsoft Internet Explorer is available free. It is
often included on computer magazine cover CDs
or it can be downloaded from
www.microsoft.com

Published by Willow Island Editions,
41 Water Lane, Middlestown,
Wakefield, WF4 4PX

www.willowisland.co.uk

ISBN 1-902467-07-8

CONTENTS

Introduction   4

The Computer   6

The Internet   13

Going Online   16

E-mail   20

Writing an e-mail message   22

Sending an e-mail message   24

Checking your e-mail   26

Surfing the Internet   28

Favourite Pages   30

Closing your Internet Session   31

Browsing   33

Whatever Next?   35

Introduction

Do you have to hold this book at arm's length to read it without your glasses?

'What book?'

Do you think of a monitor as the person in class who fills the inkwells or puts the straws in the bottles of milk at morning break, or the Net as something you used to wear at night to keep your perm in place?

If so, you may be the kind of person who feels she'll never be able to use a computer or keep up with the 'electronic age'.

You'd be wrong. You **can** do it. How many computer whiz kids can follow a knitting pattern?

If you take things step by step and make use of anyone who's prepared to show you the basics (grand-children could be particularly helpful here) you'll find a whole new world of interest and opportunity. Think how impressed your friends will be!

We hope that what follows will help you to get started, even if you've never used a computer before.

The Computer

The **computer** itself is usually inside a metal box with various slots and buttons on it and wires attached. Unless you can service a vacuum cleaner or assemble a wardrobe from a kit it is advisable to get someone to set everything up for you.

Joined to the computer box by a wire will be the **monitor**. This looks like a television set and the screen shows what is happening in the computer and displays messages, information and pictures.

Also attached to the computer is the **keyboard,** which is like a typewriter with some extra buttons on it. What you type on the keyboard is displayed on the monitor rather than on paper as it would be with a typewriter. Sometimes you have to type the answers to questions which appear on the screen.

 The computer works by using, or 'running', **programs**, some of which are already in the computer. Other programs can be loaded into the machine by inserting a CD, or compact disk, into the CD drive.

CDs are thin, flat and shiny and about the size of a saucer.

I think it must be time for a cup of tea.

The **mouse** is a plastic device which sits on a 'mouse mat' and fits into the palm of your hand. Its long tail is a wire leading into the computer. Moving the mouse on the mat causes a little arrow, or 'cursor', on the monitor screen to move around in any direction and this allows you to point at and 'select', things shown on the screen. When the cursor is in the correct position you make your selection by pushing one of the buttons (usually the left hand one) on the top of the mouse with your finger. This is called 'clicking'. Sometimes you have to do one click and sometimes two in quick succession.

CLICK!
CLICK!

At first it can be quite tricky to get the cursor to go where you want it to and to click in the right place. Simon showed me some computer games using the mouse and after practicing these for a while I got much better . . . rather like learning to knit . . . I must teach Simon how to do that.

Simon says – 'Our computer uses Microsoft Windows which has some simple card games like **Solitaire**, good for learning to 'drag' icons, position the cursor and co-ordinate clicking. Load **Solitaire** by clicking **Start** then select **Programs** – **Accessories** – **Games** and click **Solitaire**.'

The **printer** is attached to the computer by a wire and can print out what is shown on the monitor screen. You load paper into it, rather like putting paper into a typewriter, and by selecting **Print** or a little picture of a printer on the screen, using the mouse, what is on the screen will be transferred to the paper.

You may have a **scanner** attached to your computer by a wire. This enables you to copy pictures into the computer.

The **modem** connects your computer to your telephone line and is the device which makes the connection to the Internet. When sending e-mail messages, which I shall explain on Page 20, or connecting to the Internet *(Page 28)* your computer 'phones' another much bigger computer to send or receive the information. Your computer may have a modem inside it, or the modem may be added as an extra box.

Simon says – 'Don't be frightened by the names and complicated technicalities. Like your TV or car, you don't need to know how it works, just how to use it.'

The Internet

The **Internet** is a network of computers all over the world which can exchange information. You can link your computer to this network using the modem and the phone line. This allows you to find information about almost anything you can imagine (including knitting patterns).

You can look things up as you would in an encyclopaedia, find out more about favourite T.V. programmes, check on timetables or the weather forecast or browse through department stores (without getting tired feet).

There are 'websites' on the **World Wide Web** you can visit. These are the **www.** addresses you see everywhere these days.

You can also communicate with other people sharing your interests through **newsgroups** where your questions or comments are displayed as if they were on a notice board and other people can reply. There are **chat rooms** where you can 'talk' more directly with those who are connected to the 'channel' at the same time.

Simon says – 'Remember that, unless you have free Internet time, you will be paying local telephone call charges for the time that you are connected to the Internet and this will be more expensive during peak hours.'

15

Going Online

To use the Internet you have to register with an **Internet Service Provider**. There are now many service providers who give free access to the Internet (such as **Freeserve** and **Lineone** as well as supermarkets, banks and others) in addition to those who make a charge for the service (such as **AOL** or **CompuServe**).

You will be given a CD, which is loaded into the computer to set up your Internet connection. This is something which it may be best to leave to Simon or whoever is your computer enthusiast. Once the program has been installed you will be able to use, or 'access', the Internet whenever you like. This is sometimes called 'going online'.

You will need an e-mail address in order to send messages and receive them, in the same way that your home has an address so that people can write to you. This will be something like **grandma@** followed by the name of your service provider and may end with **.co.uk**, **.com** or **.net**. You will also have a password, but this can be stored in your computer so you don't have to enter it each time you want to use e-mail.

Simon says - 'We use Microsoft's **Internet Explorer** for Internet access and **Outlook Express** for e-mail. Free Internet Service Providers receive part of the local call charge you pay to your telephone company when using the Internet and they also carry online advertising.'

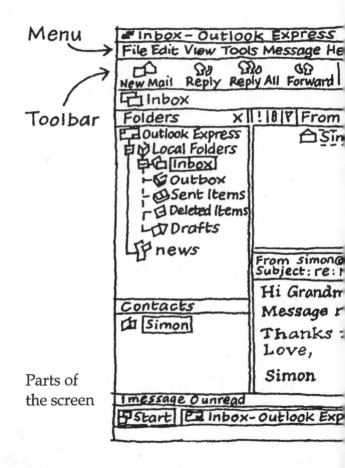

Menu

Toolbar

Parts of the screen

Inbox - Outlook Express

File Edit View Tools Message He

New Mail   Reply   Reply All   Forward

Inbox

Folders   X ! 0 ? From

Outlook Express   Si

Local Folders

Inbox

Outbox

Sent Items

Deleted Items

Drafts

news

From simon@
Subject: re:

Hi Grandm

Message r

Thanks

Love,

Simon

Contacts

Simon

1 message 0 unread

Start   Inbox - Outlook Exp

18

| | - ⊞ ✕ |

nt Delete | Send/Recv | Addresses | Find

	Received
re:My First Message	22/11/00 21:24

lowisland.co.uk to grandma@willowisland.co.uk
First Message

eived! Cool!

the Dundee cake!

|| □ working online ||

| ·s | 21.35 |

E-mail

E-mail, or electronic mail, is the computer equivalent of sending a letter. When letter-writing you find some paper and a pen, write the letter, put it in an envelope, stick a stamp on it and take it to the post box, then wait a day or two until the letter is delivered and another few days until you get a reply. With e-mail you sit at your computer and, using the mouse and the keyboard, write and deliver your 'letter' within minutes and, if the recipient checks regularly for e-mail messages, you could have a reply the same day.

It's particularly useful if you have family or friends overseas, allowing  you to keep in touch without the expense of international phone calls or the problem of time differences. It's also much quicker and cheaper than sending letters by post (or 'snail-mail', as Simon calls it).

There is an **address book** in the computer which stores e-mail addresses, so you don't have to memorise them, and when you click on an address the computer will automatically address the e-mail for you. You just type the message.

 When you send e-mail the computer will check whether any new messages are waiting for you and will pick them up.

Writing an e-mail message

☐ To:	simon@willowisland.co.uk
☐ Cc:	
Subject:	My First Message

1. After switching on the computer, select **Outlook Express**, using the mouse, by clicking twice on the left hand button. (In these instructions all 'clicks' are with the left hand button.)

2. Click once on **New Mail** in the top left hand corner of the screen and you will get a blank 'form' on the screen for composing your message.

   New Mail

3. Enter the e-mail address you are writing to in the **To** box. (Once you have some e-mail addresses in your 'address book' on the

screen you can click directly on the name you want to write to and a blank form will appear, already addressed.)

4. If you want to send a copy of your message to another e-mail address, enter this address in the **Cc** box. You move the cursor from one box to the next by pressing the **Tab** button at the left of the keyboard. Sometimes the **Tab** button is just marked with two arrows pointing in opposite directions.

5. Press **Tab** to move the cursor to the **Subject** box and type in a title for your message.

6. Press **Tab** to move the cursor to the space under these headings and type in your letter.

Sending an e-mail message

1. Click once on **Send**. This is the
   equivalent of putting the letter in
   an envelope so that it is ready to
   post and **(1)** will appear after
   Outbox on the left of the screen,
   showing that there is one
   message waiting to be sent.

2. If you have other e-mails to send,
   prepare these messages in the
   same way. The number after
   Outbox will show the number of
   messages waiting to be sent. (All
   the steps up to this point can be
   completed before you go 'online',
   or connect to the Internet.)

3. Click once on **Send/Receive**. You
   may then be shown a **Dial-up**
   Connection box, depending on
   how your computer is set up, to
   confirm that you want to go

online. Click once on **Connect**. The modem then dials and the connection is made. The messages are sent, your Outbox becomes empty and any messages waiting for you are picked up. At the bottom right of the screen a message will appear saying **No new messages** or the number of new messages received and, if there are new messages, the number will appear after **Inbox** at the left of the screen.

Simon says – 'Across the top of the screen is a **menu bar** which shows a 'drop down menu' when you click a word on the bar. Below the menu bar is a **toolbar**, with pictures. To keep things simple, Grandma only uses the toolbar.'

Checking your e-mail

1. You don't have to send e-mail in order to check whether there are any messages waiting for you. Having selected **Outlook Express** *(Page 22)* click once on **Send/Receive** *(Page 24)*. Your computer can be set to disconnect automatically after mail has been sent and received.

Send/Recv

2. New messages will be added to a list of the messages you have received already, displayed in the Inbox, preceded by a closed envelope symbol to show that they've not been opened. By clicking twice on the new message you 'open the envelope' and the full message will be displayed on your screen.

3. If you want to refer to previous messages you have received, they will be in the Inbox and messages

you have sent will be in **Sent
Items**. By clicking on them they
will be displayed on the screen
and they can be put away again by
clicking once on the cross at the
top right hand corner of the
displayed message (like keeping
your correspondence in a file).

4. If you want to reply to a message
you can click on **Reply** at the top
left of the message and a form for
Reply your reply, headed with the
recipient's address and the title
will appear, ready for you to use.

Simon says – 'If you want to alter or
add to a message which is already in
your Outbox, click on **Outbox** then click
twice on the message. The form box will
appear with your message ready to
change. To put the message back in the
Outbox you must click on **Send** again.'

Surfing the Internet

1. After switching on the computer, point to Internet Explorer, using the mouse, and click twice on the left hand button.

2. You may be shown a **Dial-up Connection** box or your computer may be set to dial automatically to your service provider. Click once on **Connect** if this box appears. The modem then dials and you will see your **home page**.

3. In the **Address** box at the top of the page will be the web address of your home page, starting **http:// www.** You can visit another website by typing the new address in this box in place of the address shown and clicking once on **Go** at the right of the box.

4. When moving the cursor over the web page on the screen the little arrow may change to a hand with a pointing finger. This shows a **link** to another web page and by clicking once on the link the new page will appear on your screen.

5. You can turn back to pages you have already visited by clicking on the **Back** arrow at the top left of the screen, or move forward again to later pages by clicking on the **Forward** arrow.

Back   Forward

Favourite Pages

Favorites (American spelling) is an
address book for websites. If a website
is listed in **Favorites** you don't have to
remember the address and you can
visit the site by clicking once on the
name. To add a website to this list you
click once on **Favorites** when viewing
the web page, then click once on **Add
to Favorites**.

If there is a page which you'd like to read at leisure 'offline' rather than during the time your computer is 'on the phone' to the Internet you save it under **Favorites** as above. There is an option box for **Make available offline** and if you click on this every page you have 'opened' on this site will be stored in your computer.

Closing your Internet Session

When you are connected to the Internet there is a little picture, or icon, of two monitors at the bottom right corner of the screen. To close your Internet session (or come offline) click twice on this icon and select **Disconnect** by clicking on this option.

Back   Forward

Viewing Offline

You can view the pages you have
stored by clicking on links or using
the **Back** and **Forward** arrows (see
Page 29). If you click on a link you
haven't visited when online you will
get a message asking if you wish to
connect again.

Printing a Web Page

To print a web page click
once on **Print** at the top of
the screen.

Browsing

If you don't have a particular website in mind, you can look for websites relating to a subject, rather like looking in a library catalogue. You do this by clicking once on **Search**, which is an option shown on your toolbar while you are using Internet Explorer. You will be shown a box which says **Find a web page containing** and you then type in 'knitting' or whatever topic you want to look for.

Click on the **Search** button next to the box and a list of sites will appear on the screen. You can click on each of these until you find something of interest, like looking through a magazine of articles about your subject. If you find there is a huge number of websites you can type in a more specific subject, such as 'knitting patterns'.

When you have finished browsing don't forget to click on the cross in the top right corner of the screen and then select **Disconnect** to close your Internet connection.

Simon says – 'You can practice finding a website by looking for

http://www.bbc.co.uk

You will find plenty of links to try out.'

Whatever Next?

We hope that you have been encouraged to take your first step into the world of computers. It is likely that in the not too distant future many of us will be using home computers and the Internet to do our shopping and banking, to book holidays and travel and as the first place we turn to for information. Television, telephone and computer may be combined in a single portable machine.

There are many books which will help you to develop your understanding of computers and you may find a course for beginners in your area. Perhaps you could create a family tree using a program designed to do this or you could even set up a family website.

... and if you need a break from all your hi-tech activities, there's always the knitting ...

'Thanks Grandma'